PROBLEM-SOLVING

D1458002

THE CAREER SKILLS LIBRARY

PROBLEM-SOLVING

by Dandi Daley Mackall

A New England Publishing Associates Book

Copyright ©1998 by Ferguson Publishing Company, Chicago, Illinois

Printed in the United States of America
U-8

Library of Congress Cataloging-in-Publication Data

Mackall, Dandi Daley.
    Problem-solving / by Dandi Daley Mackall.
        p. cm.
    Includes bibliographical references and index.
    ISBN 0-89434-210-X
    1. Problem solving. 2. Vocational guidance. 3. Career development.
    4. High school graduates—Employment. I. Title
    HD30.29.M33   1998
    650.1—dc21   97-26633
                                            CIP

CONTENTS

INTRODUCTION

There are not many things we can count on in this changing world. But one thing is for certain: We'll always have problems to solve.

You solve problems every day of your life. Without realizing it, you've probably stacked up quite a few problem-solving skills.

For example, say you plan to take the bus to school, but you miss it. You know you're in trouble. And that's one problem-solving skill—the ability to identify the problem.

Immediately you consider your options. You could walk the five miles. You could take your bicycle or roller skates. Your friend might pick you up; you could ask your mom or dad, or you could skip school. Coming up with lots of possible solutions is another problem-solving skill.

Maybe you decide the best solution is to use your mom's car. But you run into another problem. Your brother has asked for the car first. You strike a deal with him. You agree to help him practice his tennis serve on Saturday. He agrees to let you drive to school this morning. You've used another problem-solving skill—negotiation.

You dash to the car (you can still make it to school on time), jump in, and turn the key in the ignition. Nothing happens. The car won't start. You consider the possibilities and form a theory that the problem may be caused by a weak battery. Mom is famous for leaving the inside car light on. Sure enough. You check it out and find the light still turned on. You've successfully researched, formed a hypothesis, and confirmed your theory—all problem-solving skills.

Now you can fix the problem with another problem-solving skill—the action plan. You pull out the jumper cables and jump start the car. In minutes you're on your way, thanks to problem-solving skills you didn't even know you possessed.

FACTOID:
On many employee evaluation forms, the category "Problem-solving Abilities" takes up more room than any other evaluated trait.

Employers are seeking people who can handle the minor irritations and the major problems that are a part of every business. What do you do when a customer comes to you with a problem? Can you help when your work team runs into production problems? Could you help save your company from losing its competitive edge?

No matter where your career leads, you'll move faster and higher up the ladder of success if you're perceived as an effective problem solver.

---

10 PROBLEMS YOU MAY HAVE HAD BEFORE YOU LEFT HOME TODAY

► Alarm didn't go off.

► You fell back to sleep.

► Sister hogged the bathroom.

► No milk.

► Nothing for lunch (and school lunch sounds horrible).

► Mother misunderstood your comment about orange juice.

► Toothpaste isn't the sex appeal kind.

► Your favorite shirt is too wrinkled to wear.

► Shoelace breaks.

► You forgot your homework.

This book will help you take those innate problem-solving skills a step further. We'll go on an intriguing exploration into your brain to discover how you think. Then we'll look at a simple five-step process to help you solve problems and make decisions.

With a little effort, you can become an expert problem solver. No problem.

PART ONE
PROBLEM-SOLVING TOOLS

CHAPTER ONE
THE PROBLEM IS...

In Los Angeles, California, a luxurious high-rise apartment building was on the brink of bankruptcy. Tenant after tenant turned in their notice and moved out. To owners of the building, the mass exodus made no sense. Their beautiful, well-kept apartments offered a sound bargain in a safe neighborhood. So why were people abandoning what should have been a renter's paradise?

The building corporation hired a problem-solving group to get to the bottom of the mystery. After interviewing residents and former apartment dwellers, the problem-solving team presented its findings: People were moving out because the apartment elevators were too slow.

A team of troubleshooters was flown in to solve the problem. They gathered cost and labor estimates on several options from repairing the old elevators or putting in new ones. But every option proved too expensive.

Defeated, the building corporation had just about decided to sell or destroy the building, when the youngest member of the corporation took a creative look at the problem. The real problem, he suggested, wasn't the elevators. The real problem was that tenants got bored waiting for the elevators. His solution? Pipe music into the elevators. Cover elevator interiors with mirrors and add mirrored panels to all waiting areas.

His creative solution worked. The tenants, busy primping or examining themselves in the mirrors, soothed by elevator music, quit complaining. The exodus ceased. The building was saved. And one creative problem solver had made his mark.

No matter what job you take, not a day will pass without some kind of problem. Certain basic skills can equip you to turn those problems into opportunities. Become a problem solver where you work, and you'll make yourself an asset to the company.

Some people make things happen. Some people watch things happen, and some people say, "What happened?"
                                        —Casey Stengel

14

(Courtesy: Prints & Photographs Division, Library of Congress)

As a player on the Boston Braves, Casey Stengel watched how his manager solved the countless problems that arose during each baseball game. His later career as one of the most successful managers in baseball history was based on the problem-solving skills he learned on the field.

(Joe Duffy)

EVERYDAY PROBLEMS

Solving problems isn't something new for you. Think of how many problems you had to solve this week.

► What should I wear to school?

► My jeans are dirty. What should I wear now?

► How will I get to school?

► Should I get a date for Friday night? How? Who?

► Where can I find a ride to the dentist?

► My club (church group, team or community group) needs to raise money or plan an event.

► The car is almost out of gas, and I'm broke.

► Somebody's in my usual seat in English class.

16

- ▶ I didn't pack a lunch, and they're serving meat loaf.
- ▶ No legal parking spots available.
- ▶ I don't understand the chemistry assignment.
- ▶ My French teacher has an attitude.
- ▶ My buddy and I had a misunderstanding.
- ▶ The computer won't work.
- ▶ My CD player is not working.
- ▶ I'm locked out of the house.
- ▶ They delivered the wrong pizza.
- ▶ I'm getting a D in history.
- ▶ I have practice after school and a report due tomorrow.
- ▶ It's my move in chess (or checkers, Sega, poker, etc.).

Because you solve these problems regularly, chances are you don't even realize the complex processes involved. Yet each of the above problems requires a degree of problem-solving skill. When you figured out what to do in each case, you had to size up the problem. You considered your options. Maybe you had to negotiate. Finally, you came up with a solution and did something. Those are all problem-solving skills you'll need on the job.

17

PROBLEM-SOLVING SKILLS YOU ALREADY USE

▶ Identify the problem
▶ Negotiate
▶ Brainstorm many options
▶ Select the best option
▶ Think creatively
▶ Think logically
▶ Analyze the problem
▶ Research
▶ Form a hypothesis
▶ Troubleshoot

PROBLEM-SOLVING SKILLS ON THE JOB

What kinds of problem-solving skills do employers expect you to have? In Pittsburgh, Pennsylvania, over 1,000 high school classrooms display a chart titled: What Do Employers Expect of Me as an Employee? Ten employer expectations follow. At the top of the list is: "Recognize problems and find solutions." The last expectation is the only one in red ink: "Read, write and calculate well."

Tonya got her first real job with a major airline as soon as she graduated from college. She didn't realize what a good problem solver she was until her first job evaluation. Tonya's review included these comments:

Very resourceful—thinks of creative
   ways to solve problems.

Handles obstacles conscientiously.

Generates alternative solutions when
   solving problems.

Tonya says she learned to solve problems on high school committees and on backstage crews of community theater productions. "I was the one behind the scenes, holding things together. I never got a part in a play, but I put scenery together. And if the spotlight didn't work, I'd figure something out. If we needed stairs or a window for a set and didn't have them, I'd manage to improvise."

Tonya hadn't been working at the airline long before coworkers discovered her problem-solving skills. "People started coming to me with little problems. I'd fix them. But this time, they noticed. I got a reputation as a problem solver."

Jared's first job was with a food service company in New Jersey. He took the position because he needed the money, and he liked the hours. He had no idea that the company's problems had anything to do with him personally. After six months, Jared received his first employee evaluation:

(Courtesy: Delta Air Lines)

Your learning experiences during school can help prepare you for solving on-the-job problems. After carefully analyzing the situation, you may have to improvise to quickly find a solution for a customer or co-worker.

Jared isn't alert to problems.

Can't handle complex problems or identify key issues.

Slow to take action.

Needs to be persistent in problem solving.

Seldom generates more than one solution to a problem.

Jared admits he deserved the poor rating. He explains, "If a customer came to me with a problem, my standard answer was, 'That's not my responsibility.' Maybe I'd tell the customer to ask somebody else. If our division didn't meet production standards, it wasn't my fault. Not my problem, I thought."

Jared's evaluation woke him up to the importance of becoming a problem solver. He started paying closer attention to his company and his customers. He began to take on problems he hadn't considered his responsibility before. And Jared's next evaluation turned out much better.

PROBLEM SOLVERS

J. R. Richmond, a Midwest retailer for 40 years, believes he can tell what kind of career someone will have by the way he or she approaches a problem. Richmond divides would-be problem solvers into five groups:

1. Not my problem. These employees ignore customers and company problems as if those problems didn't touch them personally. If they do manage to get a job, they probably won't keep it long.

2. Don't ask me. Some people can't do simple calculations, keep a checkbook, a receipt record, or do basic math. Few employers have the time or means to teach these basic skills.

3. What now? Some well-meaning employees can't seem to mature into independent problem

solvers. They distrust their own judgment. As a result, they bother somebody every two minutes with a problem too big for them to handle. If these employees don't change, they may annoy themselves out of a job.

4. <u>Straight liner.</u> Straight liners know how to solve straightforward problems. They can do math and calculations and may be highly skilled professionals. But if the situation requires a new solution or any creativity, they can't handle it. They may keep their job and find a comfortable place in the company. But they shouldn't expect to advance to high levels of management.

5. <u>Creative problem solver.</u> Businesses will always have spots for people who can use their creativity to solve problems. Creative problem solvers make themselves irreplaceable.

Mimi Silbert grew up in a small flat in one of the poorest parts of Boston. Somehow she made her way through college and into a secure job as a therapist. She says, "As far as I can remember, I was always the person that everybody called with their problems. My job was to mediate and solve them."

But after a time, solving problems on a small scale as a therapist didn't seem enough. Ms. Silbert wanted to find a way to help more people out of poverty. She didn't believe the assumptions of others, that ex-criminals couldn't be taught values and integrity, along with job skills.

She started by taking applications from people who could barely fill out the forms. Next, she trained people who trained people, who... And since 1971, over 12,000 people have found success through the Delancy Street program out of San Francisco. Thousands of the nation's most "unproductive" people have become contributing members of a working community because Mimi Silbert knew how to look at an old problem in a new way.

F A C T O I D :

Some corporations prefer to hire successful bridge, chess, backgammon, or poker players over college grads because they understand the risk associated with moves and have developed skills to succeed in corporate environments.

It's up to you which kind of problem solver you'll become. If you start now to develop your problem-solving skills, your ability to come up with logical and

Confident of your problem-solving skills, you can turn each problem into an opportunity.

creative solutions could form the foundation of a successful career. Confident of your problem-solving skills, you can turn each problem into an opportunity.

EXERCISE

1. List 10 problems you solved today. What problem-solving skills did you use?

2. When you have a major problem, is there somebody you go to for help? What is it about that person that makes you think he can handle the problem?

3. Describe the biggest problem facing you right now. What skills will you need to solve it?

2 CHAPTER TWO
SCIENTIFIC THINKING

The best tool you have at your disposal for solving problems is your head. Problem solving begins with clear thinking. And thinking comes in two basic varieties: (1) scientific and (2) creative.

Scientific thinking goes by many names: logical, critical, analytical, convergent, straight-line, predictable thinking. It follows certain rules of logic from Point A through Point B to Point C. Scientific thinking marches you through a hypothesis to the right answer.

Scientific thinking marches you through a hypothesis to the right answer.

Creative thinking has other names, too: inspirational, divergent, insightful, exploratory, unpredictable thinking. Creative thinking skyrockets you through new, provocative channels to shed light on new answers to old problems.

You need both powers of thought every day. Where do these different kinds of thinking come from? The different hemispheres of your brain.

USING YOUR BRAIN

Your brain has two sides. Each side controls certain body and thinking functions. The left side of the brain is in charge of analytical thinking, logic. It takes you through well-ordered steps and makes you the genius you are in math.

The right side operates in images and impressions, rather than numbers and words. Creativity and art originate in the right brain. The chart on page 27 shows how the two sides of your brain divide and conquer the unfathomable task of thinking you through life.

Good problem solvers need to draw on both sides of the brain. The young, corporate executive in the last chapter, who solved the problem of slow elevators by installing mirrors and music, used his creative right brain. But if the elevator is broken, you'll need the scientific left brain to get to the bottom of the problem and fix it.

FACTOID:

In most people the right hemisphere of the brain controls the muscles of and receives information from the left half of the body and vice versa. And, by the time a person is 50, the brain shrinks slightly, losing about an ounce in weight.

RIGHT- AND LEFT-BRAIN COMPARISONS

Left Brain	Right Brain
Seeks one right answer	Explores, seeks, examines from many viewpoints
Recognizes words	Recognizes facts or objects
Processes one stimulus at a time at lightning speed	Processes whole clusters of stimuli all at once
Orderly sequences of thought	Grasps complex wholes
A focus on parts	Takes in whole picture
Logical	Dreams
Linear thinking	Makes sense by discovering workable patterns
Organizes into units	Can connect parts of the world into fresh patterns
Governed by rules, plays by rules	Follows few rules
Draws on learned, fixed codes	Can deal with new information where no learned program is available
Organized	Sees correspondences or resemblances
Can recall complex motor sequences	Thinks in complex images
Best in implementing programs after setup	Best in initial orientation of a task

MATH IS MATH

Scientific thinking is best used when the problem requires one answer. So, a lot of scientific problem solving can be done with solid math and calculation skills. Maria says she owes her employment with a large Midwest manufacturer to what she learned in math classes at school. She explains: "To apply for my position, I had to take a Class II test that looked like my junior high math quizzes. My boss says I'd be shocked by how many applicants fail the test."

EXCERPT FROM A MANUFACTURER'S APPLICATION TEST

1. Reduce these fractions to their lowest terms:
   A. $^{10}/_{32}$ = _____
   B. $^{72}/_{128}$ = _____
   C. $^{19}/_{64}$ = _____

2. Subtract these fractions and reduce the answers to the lowest terms:
   A. $9^{14}/_{16} - 5^{6}/_{16}$ = _____
   B. $7^{14}/_{16} - 4^{6}/_{16}$ = _____

3. Add these decimals:
   A. $1.47 + 16.235 + 7.16 + .21$ = _____
   B. $10.245 + .479 + .2 + 4.1$ = _____

4. Convert these decimals to fractions:
   A. $.0938$ = _____
   B. $.2656$ = _____
   C. 1.32 = _____

Maria's starting job was on an assembly line. Her boss wanted to make sure she had the thinking skills she'd need if a problem did arise.

Ryan's ability to estimate cost and draw up a budget pushed him to the top of his training group his first year with a Texas investment firm. He explains where he acquired his skills. "I guess I started when I was eight years old and got my first allowance. Before I spent a penny, I'd write down how much I'd spend on gum, how much on candy and how much I'd save for some great thing I wanted. I did the same kind of cost estimate when I was our high school prom committee chairperson." Ryan had used his analytical thinking skills as a student and reaped the benefit in his career.

FOUR STEPS TO CRITICAL THINKING

Analytical or critical thinking travels through four basic steps:

Step 1. Identify the problem and break it down.

Step 2. Collect information, research.

Step 3. Form opinions (hypothesis).

Step 4. Draw conclusions.

How does the process work? Try this scenario. What would you do?

One afternoon 50 students at your high school come down with stomach cramps and vomiting. All of them ate the school lunch—hot dogs. Those who didn't eat school lunch, didn't get sick. What do you conclude?

If you already decided it was the hot dogs, think again, Sherlock. Use your scientific thinking skills instead of jumping to the obvious conclusion.

Step 1: Identify the problem. Kids are sick and you want to find out what caused the problem.

Step 2: Collect information. Investigate. So you found out that the hot dog eaters got sick and the brown baggers didn't. Keep going. Ask questions to get you to the end before you leap there. Did some students who ate hot dogs not end up vomiting? Did they all have mustard or ketchup or relish? Did something else come with the hot dogs, like chips or pickles? Were all the sickies from the same lunch period?

Expand your research to the kitchen. Did the same cafeteria server handle hamburgers and hot dogs? Did only one server handle the dogs? Anybody sick back in the kitchen? Are there any toxic substances near the hot dog preparation area? Check out the hot dog oven. What about pans and serving platters? Anybody examine those hot dog buns? Are there uncooked hot

30

(Joe Duffy)

dogs lying around? Never shortcut the information-gathering step in a scientific investigation.

Step 3: Form your hypothesis. Maybe, after all your investigations, you still blame the hot dog. In your opinion, the hot dog is responsible for student sickness that afternoon. That's your theory, your hypothesis.

Step 4: Draw your conclusions. You can't do that until you test your hypothesis, right? If you're brave, you might run your own experiment and eat one of the suspect hot dogs. Or, you could whip out your junior detective set and run a substance analysis on it. The fourth step is the time to test your theory and confirm your hypothesis or adjust your conclusion.

So, you eat the hot dog, but you don't get sick. You examine the meat under your microscope, but you come up clean. Just regulation pig guts. It's time to consider a new hypothesis. Since only one person prepared the hot dogs, and he didn't touch the hamburgers, you shift your suspicions to him. To test your new theory, you spy on him. Sure enough, you see him cough without covering his mouth. The man confesses that he just got over the flu. Case solved.

START NOW

What can you do now to develop your scientific thinking? Plenty. Take math and science, for one thing. Start budgeting your personal finances. Try going through the four steps of critical thinking the next time you have a problem that needs *the* answer. And the next time you see the love of your life talking to somebody new, don't jump to conclusions. Use your scientific thinking skills to investigate.

EXERCISE

1. Which of the following problems can best be solved through scientific thinking?

   a. You plan to buy a new car and don't know which car to get.

   b. You've made a date to go to the drive-in on Saturday night, but you don't have a car.

   c. You have to drive to the orthodontist's right after school and you don't know the fastest way to get there.

Answer: a and c require scientific thinking. By gathering information, you should be able to arrive at the best car for you—one best answer. And, although many roads lead to the orthodontist's office, only one route is fastest. (As far as your carless drive-in date, you're going to need as much creativity as possible to get you out of that one.)

2. Pretend you're buying a new car. Use the four-step scientific method. Write a sentence or two describing what you'll do for each stage.

3 CHAPTER THREE
CREATIVE
THINKING

Now it's time to get creative. For which of the following problems will you need to apply a hefty dose of right-brained, creative thinking?

1. Your graduating class needs to come up with a class motto.

2. You don't know where to take your date on Friday night.

3. You need a prom theme.

4. You didn't do your homework, and you need an excuse fast.

Answer? All of the above. Creative thinking explores the possibilities. It examines the problem from as many angles as possible. When you need lots of ideas—for a class motto, a date, a prom theme, or a homework excuse—you need creative or divergent thinking.

THINKING OUTSIDE THE DOTS

Try this universal thinking exercise. Make nine dots on a sheet of paper. Without lifting your pencil, can you draw four straight lines to connect the dots? See the answer on page 46.

Most people can't solve the dot problem because they restrict themselves in their thought processes. They don't allow themselves to go outside the dots. Rather than taking you in a direct path of thought, creative thinking takes you off that beaten path, hopefully to a place where no person has trod.

The significant problems we face cannot be solved at the same level of thinking we were at when we created them.

—**Albert Einstein**

(Courtesy: Prints & Photographs division, Library of Congress)

Albert Einstein recognized that searching for solutions to new problems required breaking free from old thought patterns.

Creative thinking is called in when you need new solutions to old problems. Imagine this. It's the day you've dreaded. You have to get up in front of your entire second-period class and give a report on coal mining in Newcastle. You're prepared. But in the hall on your way to class, you catch the hem of your dress (or your shirt that can't possibly be tucked in), and the hem pulls out. You have to fix it, but there's no needle, no thread. What would you do?

Needle and thread would have been easy. Now you have to think outside the dots. Without reading further, see how many ideas you can come up with.

Okay. Here are some possibilities to use in repairing your hem: staple, tape, pin, paper clip, string, safety pin, bobby pin, barrette, brads, garbage bag ties, paste, glue, jelly, gum, peanut butter, melted Snickers, or you could trade clothes with a friend.

With a little creative thinking, the possibilities are endless.

FACTOID:

You don't have to have a high IQ to be a good thinker. Psychologist E. Paul Torrance has shown that fully 70% of all creative people score below 135 on IQ tests.

Marcella is a second-year shipping clerk who believes in the power of creative thinking. "In high school, nobody especially thought of me as creative. But when our class was in charge of homecoming, the prom, or our senior trip, I always had a lot of ideas to offer." When she graduated, Marcella took a job that involved supplying large companies with stationery and other office supplies.

Marcella says her habit of coming up with a lot of

ideas quickly made her an asset. "I discovered that shipping clerks had to get creative when supply didn't exactly meet demand. When we ran short of green pens, I'd think of options to the usual slow back-order notification: call the customer and apologize, give a discount on another color, offer to send what we had. Pretty soon, I was the "Idea Woman."

Marcella had developed her own techniques for creative thinking. And her creativity secured her job.

TECHNIQUES FOR BREAKTHROUGH THINKING

If your thinking is in a rut (and even if it's not), try the techniques discussed in the following sections for sparking creativity.

No great discovery is ever made without a bold guess.
                              —Sir Isaac Newton

Brainstorming

Brainstorming is the process of rapidly spilling out every idea imaginable. Chapter 7 will deal in greater detail with methods of brainstorming. But for now, imagine your boss has asked you to come up with a new name for your product. No scientific thought will discover the answer. You need to come up with as many possibilities as you can think of. Then you can choose the best one.

Asking questions

THE CAT

It's obvious that these letters spell out "THE CAT," right? But take a closer look. The H and A are the same. But you saw what you expected to see in the example adapted from O. G. Selfridge's *Pattern Recognition and Modern Computers*.

Don't accept everything at face value. Challenge assumptions.

When you hit a problem, make sure you're seeing it clearly. Asking questions can be a great way of stirring your creative thoughts. Don't accept everything at face value. Challenge assumptions.

Suppose your teacher tells the class that because there has been too much talking, you must all decide your own punishment. But while the rest of the class is trying to devise weak forms of punishment, you ask questions.

Was there too much talking? How about compared to other classes? What's too much anyway? Who did the talking? Why were they talking? What kind of talking? And why was talking so bad anyway? Would it have been okay if the teacher had talked with them? If people had talked on the "right" subject? What if the class had designated talking breaks, 60 seconds when you could talk to anybody about anything? That wouldn't be too much, would it? Is talking the real problem? What if the teacher...?

Of course, there's a time to keep your questions to yourself and a wise person knows when. But you can cultivate the art of questioning all day long.

Turning Things Upside Down

When everybody else is analyzing a problem in the same way and getting nowhere, turn the whole thing upside down. Kevin works on a manufacturing team that is responsible for producing a set number of pump parts per week. When his team failed to meet its goal four weeks in a row, the team met to try to solve the problem.

Kevin explains what happened next. "We went round and round and got nowhere. First, we looked at our own performance, but we knew we couldn't

(Courtesy: Vinal Regional Vocational Technical School, Middletown, CT)

Working together as a team enables you to recognize the problem, find a solution and accomplish your original goal.

go any faster. Our boss suggested we might have to get higher-power equipment to get the pieces out of the plant faster."

That's when Kevin turned the whole thing upside down. "Instead of looking at us or the machinery, I looked at our spread table [where pieces were placed for assembly]. All of a sudden it hit me. If we had an L-shaped table, we could cut out one step. Nobody had ever thought of it before."

Kevin's team made its goal with an afternoon to spare. Their boss rewarded the team's creativity by

42

letting them go home early every Friday, as long as they'd reached their production goal.

The Ever-present Notebook

Creative thinking doesn't always come on demand. Some of the world's best ideas have come in odd places, like bathtubs and under apple trees. It's a good idea to carry a small notebook around with you. At least keep a notepad by your bedside, in the car, and next to the shower. Too often that right brain clicks in when you're least prepared. Don't miss your best ideas simply because you didn't write them down.

Keep a notepad by your bedside, in the car and next to the shower.

Visualizing

Visualizing is a technique we'll talk more about later. Your creative mind can take in the whole, big picture. Try picturing how things will look when your problem is solved. You want a pet, but you don't know which pet to get. Can you visualize yourself in your room, happy with your...what? Your iguana? Your cat, dog, snake, camel? But you better combine your creative thinking with scientific thinking before you make your purchase.

Visualizing, or imaging, may give you the edge to come up with that multimillion-dollar new product. Can't you picture designer water for dogs? All the shelves right above the dog food in your local super-market stacked with rows of your creation, "Pure Puppy" or is it "Doggie Dew"?

No two problems are alike. Try a different point of view. Be radical. For years companies tried to cut employee insurance expenses. They explored cheaper health-care providers, poorer coverage, higher co-payments. Then one executive turned the whole thing upside down. Why not work on getting employees in better health? Then they won't need so much care. They built an exercise room and started company weight-loss bonus programs. Medical costs went down.

CREATIVITY AND YOU

So you think you're not the creative type. You're just not artsy-craftsy. Well, think again. True, some people are more creative than others. But we all start out with a degree of creativity. Young children are curious by nature. They ask questions and come up with wild ideas. They can imagine what it might be like to fly like a bird or sit on a cloud.

Now is the time to recapture that child-like curiosity. Have some fun. Let yourself be ridiculous. Ask 20 questions a day about things you've always taken for granted. Why do clocks run clockwise? Why are there only nine numbers and a zero to work with? Why is bacon cut in strips? Why don't they make a microwave cooling appliance to freeze things instantly?

The man who asked himself as he drove home in a light drizzle, "Why don't they make windshield wipers that pause for light rain?" is a millionaire today. He took his idea (and his patent) to automobile manufacturers and cashed it in.

At your new job, your very newness may be an asset. You may come in with just the fresh point of view your team needs. Don't be intimidated. Of course, you need to respect experience. They may already have tried your idea. But maybe not. Don't waste a creative idea because you're afraid they won't like it. Open your mind to all the possibilities.

EXERCISE

1. Come up with 20 questions about things you've never stopped to wonder about.
2. Turn your bedroom upside down—not literally. Imagine as many ways as possible to rearrange your room.
3. It's snowing. You have to get to school, and there are no shoes or boots in the house. Improvise. Make a list of things you could wear.

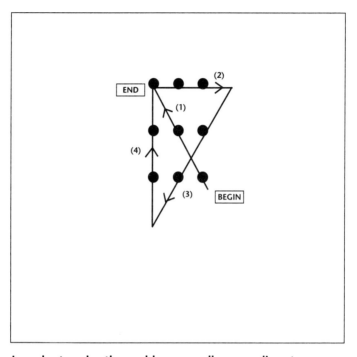

In order to solve the problem, you allow your lines to pass through the center and sides of dots and let the lines extend beyond the box of dots.

CHAPTER FOUR
POTHOLES AND PITFALLS

"**B**uy our toothpaste and improve your love life."

"Before I called Psychic Hotline, I was bankrupt. Now that I'm in contact with my personal psychic, I've just made my first million. Call for yourself and get rid of financial worries."

"If you don't send your contribution in today, our station may go off the air. And thousands of little children will never know true joy."

"Want your child to stay warm in the cold, outside world? Make him warm on the inside. Give him oatmeal."

"Double your pleasure. Double your fun. Chew our gum."

What's wrong with these promises? They have helped sell millions of dollars in products and services. Some of them sound pretty good. Who wouldn't want to make a million bucks *and* have sex appeal?

But you know better. You sense something's not quite on the up-and-up. But what? Can you pick out the exact place where these promises go wrong? Each one contains at least one error in logic. We call those wrong turns in thinking "logical fallacies."

LOGICAL FALLACIES

On the surface it makes sense that if Jolene called a psychic and got inside information that turned her into a millionaire, you could do the same. But the logic is false. Her financial success may have had nothing to do with the tip from her psychic. And even if it did, who says the same thing can happen to you?

All the facts aren't in on toothpaste and gum either. There may be more to those stories of sex appeal and pleasure. And what exactly does oatmeal have to do with keeping a kid warm as he trudges through the snow to get the school bus? Again, even if the TV station does fold because I fail to send in my contribution, couldn't those kids find joy somewhere else?

We get ourselves (and our employers) into trouble when we take a wrong turn in thinking and follow a logical fallacy. If you're aware of the pitfalls and logical potholes out there, then you'll have a better chance of avoiding them.

"NOT SO FAST"

Which of these two lines is longer?

If you're like most people, you assumed A was longer than B. The truth is A and B are the same length. Line A looked longer at first glance. You needed to investigate and remain open to avoid the logical pitfall.

Marlene admits she fell for the "not-so-fast" fallacy more than once in high school. "I always ended up with the wrong boyfriend, for one thing," she says. "If a guy looked good and talked smooth, I figured he was for me. I wish somebody had been around to tell me, 'Not so fast.'"

But by the time Marlene joined her first work team in a real estate office, she had learned her lesson. "Even though the first day I thought I had everybody figured out, I held back. I'd finally learned I couldn't tell a book by its cover." Marlene learned to check potential buyers out and research her facts. "Sometimes a buyer will tell me money is no problem. He looks the part of a wealthy tycoon and sounds sincere. But when I check my facts, I find out he's not what he claimed."

49

Check your facts, too. Before you recommend or do business with another person, business, or agency, tell yourself, "Not so fast." Then use your logical thinking skills to find out what you need to know.

Tyrone learned to hate the way his college acquaintances stereotyped him. He explains: "I attended an out-of-state university because they had a good journalism school and I had relatives close by. But because I'm African American and tall, the first question I'd get asked when they found out I was from out of state was, 'Are you here on a basketball scholarship?' Like there wasn't any other reason I'd be there."

Those students who stereotyped Tyrone were guilty of a "not-so-fast" logical fallacy. And that can be the basis of misunderstanding and prejudice. Don't assume things about your coworkers on the basis of racial, gender, ethnic or cultural backgrounds. Don't assume you know what someone likes or dislikes because you think all women do or a certain nationality doesn't.

RUSH TO JUDGMENT

You've cruised through your first-quarter geometry class with a B. Second quarter your teacher takes a leave of absence and a substitute takes over the class.

Six weeks later your parents get a warning slip with your name on it. You're failing geometry. "It's Ms. Trapezoid's fault!" you plea. "I was doing fine until she took over. They should get rid of her. Give *her* the warning slip!"

Makes sense. But don't rush to judgment. There could be many explanations for your lower grade. This quarter's material could be harder. Or, you may have been goofing off because she's just a sub. Or maybe your first teacher never graded anything and gave you all Bs. You'll never know by rushing to the easiest answer. You need to logically check the facts.

People in the business world get fired all the time because companies panic and rush to judgment. The new CEO comes in and profits drop. Out goes the new CEO, even if there are better explanations for the profit loss.

Investigate before you rush to judgment.

The same thing happens in the world of sports. Coaches and managers better win, or they're out of a job. Never mind that the owner of the team has lost the best players by refusing to raise salaries.

Be careful of the connections you make in your business dealings. Investigate before you rush to judgment.

*The first problem for all of us, men and
women, is not to learn, but to unlearn.*
                                    —Gloria Steinem

HASTY GENERALIZATION

Kathy is failing history. Alfred is failing history. Even
Zack, Brad, and Angela are failing history. Therefore,
nobody can pass that history class.

That's a hasty generalization. First, maybe somebody is passing and you just don't know about it.
Second, so what if nobody's passing. You could be
the first!

Kyle says he comes by his stubborn nature honestly,
having inherited it from stubborn parents who taught
him not to give up. He remembers a time in high
school when he refused to give in to a hasty generalization. "My graduating class was small. We wanted to
go on a senior trip together for a week. All my friends
said the school would never let us. The class ahead of
us didn't take one. As far back as we knew, no class
had been allowed an overnight senior trip."

But Kyle refused to accept the generalization that
nobody could do it. "Three of us presented our case
to the board of education. They said yes. We spent a
glorious week in the Ozarks."

(Courtesy: Gloria Steinem)

As author and feminist Gloria Steinem has pointed out,
before you learn something new, you may have to "unlearn"
something old.

Kyle took his determination with him to San Francisco, where he joined a public relations team. His first account was a soft drink company who wanted to get a foothold in the area. "Just because Coke couldn't do it and Pepsi couldn't do it, that didn't mean we couldn't. I'd at least try and find out for myself."

POISONING THE WELL

Poisoning the well is the logical fallacy that will keep you from making your own, untainted decisions about individuals, ideas, or even companies. Instead of making up your own mind, you listen to the negative comments of someone else and allow those comments to color your logic.

I mistrust the judgment of every man in a case in which his own wishes are concerned.

—The Duke of Wellington

Eric fell into this logical pothole as a sophomore in high school, but it taught him a lesson he took with him to his first job. He chose the wrong Spanish teacher. "All my friends told me to stay away from Mr. H. He gave quizzes. He doled out homework. So when I was assigned to his room, I never gave him a chance. I dropped his class and took somebody else the next semester. But I still regret it. I didn't learn anything in the other class. And the kids in Mr. H's class did."

During Eric's first month at his new job, he sensed a power struggle between his team leader and their supervisor. "Before I even met the supervisor, my team leader warned me about her: she's bossy, tough to work with. But this time I decided I'd give the supervisor a chance and decide for myself. Turned out she was tough, but she was fair."

CAR WASHING IN THE RAIN

This is one logical fallacy that's all around you. "Every time I wash my car, it rains. I'm not washing it Saturday. I don't want the big game rained out." "Whenever Macey comes along on our picnics, we all end up fighting. Let's not invite her." "This is my lucky shirt. If I don't wear it for the match, I'll lose." "She reads all the time, and now she needs glasses. No way I'm going to read."

The fancy name for this logical fallacy is *ex post facto* reasoning. Because B happened after A, A must have caused B. Again, be careful about your connections. A cause and effect are more complicated than one event following another. Presidents are quick to make a connection between their presidency and a growing economy: "Since I became president, the gross national product is up!" But if the economy goes down, they claim there's no connection.

A cause and effect are more complicated than one event following another.

Be careful. Just because your office has had problems since Harry joined the team, it might not be poor Harry's fault.

"YOU JUST GOTTA"

"Please, please! You just gotta pass me in the course. If you don't, I won't graduate. If I don't graduate, I

(Joe Duffy)

can't go to college and my mom will die. And I'll end up with no job, no home, no future."

That's the emotional, "you just gotta," logical fallacy. If an ex-love wants to come back to you "...because I can't live without you," check your logic. Sort out fact from emotion. You were still cheated on and lied to. Right?

Emotional arguments will come at you from all directions throughout your career. Don't lose your compassion, but don't fall into an emotional pitfall of logic either. Your coworker may urge you to lie for him because the boss will fire him if the truth comes out. Another coworker may plead with you to back

her up on her proposal in a team meeting. After all,
look at all she's done for you and what good friends
you are. Sort out the emotions. Handle the matter
and people involved with tact and compassion. But
think and act with logic.

LOGICAL FALLACIES

Not so fast	"He'll like this. All guys do."
Rush to judgment	"She's a good dresser. Let's hire her."
Hasty generalization	"Everybody else goes. We better go, too."
Poisoning the well	"Don't listen to him. I heard he lies."
Car washing in the rain	"Fire her. We haven't made a sale since she got here."
"You just gotta"	"You just gotta give me a raise or they'll repossess my car!"

THINKING AIDS

To help you avoid the pitfalls and potholes of logical
fallacies, here's a check list of thinking aids:

▶ Don't go for the easy answer. Do your homework. Just because Disneyland is a hit in
   California and Florida doesn't guarantee success
   for Euro-Disney.

▶ Make good connections. Don't assume a cause-and-effect relationship. Investigate to discover the real explanations for successes and failures.

▶ Know the difference between fact and opinion. Even if an authority or expert gives you an opinion, check the facts.

▶ Learn to delay gratification. Don't go for the quick fix or explanation.

▶ Challenge assumptions. Are things really this way, or could you be overlooking something?

▶ Avoid the blame game. Fault and failure are rarely the result of one person's mistake. Explore deeper causes and ask "why" instead of "who."

▶ Know yourself. Don't govern your decisions on emotion. Learn from past mistakes. Try not to make the same mistake twice. Start now to build your resistance to logical fallacies.

EXERCISE

1. In between those favorite TV shows, try this. Watch television commercials and pick out the faults in their claims.

2. Think about your last argument with someone. List your main points and their main points. Now, sort out fact and opinion.

3. When you get the urge to buy something, see if you can track your own logic. What influenced your decision and desire?

THE PROBLEM-SOLVING PROCESS

THE FIVE-STEP
PROBLEM-SOLVING PROCESS

Step 1. Identify and Define the Problem

Step 2. Define Goals and Objectives

Step 3. Generate Solutions

Step 4. Make a Plan of Action

Step 5. Follow Through

5

STEP 1: IDENTIFY AND DEFINE THE PROBLEM

An age-old business saying goes like this: "Understand the problem well enough, and the solution will present itself." Don't cut short the first step in the problem-solving process. Identify and define the problem.

Take the elevator example from chapter 1. Tenants were moving out of a high-rise building that had slow elevators. As soon as one thinker identified and defined the real problem, he had his solution. The problem was tenant boredom. The solution was elevator music and mirrors.

THREE KINDS OF PROBLEMS

Although most problems are complex, it may help to divide potential problems into three groups for easier identification: people problems, organizational problems, and mechanical problems.

Correctly identifying whether your problem is rooted in people, the organization, or mechanics should help you zero in on the right solution.

People Problems

You. Imagine the kinds of problems you might run into as you start your career. That first year on the job, you may discover that you are your biggest problem. You may be unprepared for the required job skills, the stress of your new job or your new life in general.

Like Alan, who took an entry-level job with an airplane manufacturer in St. Louis, you may wish you'd taken more technical classes. After three weeks, Alan felt himself drowning in a sea of procedures and technical equipment. He and his boss agreed that Alan hadn't gotten enough training. They identified his problem. Then, with the support of his company, Alan signed up for evening classes to fill in the gaps.

Sarah felt her training had prepared her well for her job in telemarketing. What she wasn't prepared for were the pressures that accompanied her job. Her own unhappiness became her worst enemy. Unsure of the origin of her problems at work, she quit after three months.

Few new jobs match our high expectations. The actual 9 to 5 work can come as a letdown after the skyrocketing career you envisioned. The company's values might challenge your personal ethics. Disappointment in your job can prove a major obstacle to career success.

If you can narrow the vague sensation that your job isn't working out for you and identify the actual problem, you'll have a better chance at solving it.

On the other hand, unhappiness may originate at home but carry over to work. You feel lost without your old friends. This could be your first time living on your own. Personal, financial, and relationship problems follow you to work. If you know you are the problem, then you know where to look for the solution. It's not the company that needs to change—it's you.

Person Conflict. Another kind of people problem is a conflict between you and one other person. You run into a problem with a coworker—a personality clash, career jealousy, unhealthy competition. Your boss might take some getting used to. Recognizing the problem for what it is can help you handle your conflict.

Ginny discovered personality conflicts at work could prove more dangerous than conflicts in high school. "In high school, if I didn't hit it off with someone, I didn't hang out with her. If some teacher forced us to work together on a project, I knew it would all be over when the semester ended. But a personality conflict at

(V. Harlow/Me & McGees Restaurant)

If you deal with the public on a daily basis, you will have to learn how to handle customers in a way that avoids "people conflicts."

work can wreck everything. The other person doesn't just go away." Ginny had to learn how to work through the conflict to solve the problem.

Don't criticize others. They are just what we would be under similar circumstances.
                                            —Abraham Lincoln

If you can't handle a customer, a client, or a supplier, you have a people conflict. Problems with discrimination and office romances fall into this category. When two people feud, the whole team—

even the company itself—may be at risk. And if that happens, your job is at risk, too. The sooner you pinpoint the problem, the better.

When two people feud, the whole team— even the company itself— may be at risk.

Group People Problems. You may run into group problems at work. Your team's morale sinks. Or, your team gives into petty jealousies and fails to come together as a group. You may like each other, but fail to produce as a team and meet your goals and objectives.

Factions can divide a work team as one group squares off against another. Departments carry on unhealthy competition within the company. Management and labor do battle. A good problem solver has to be on the alert for any of these potential people problems.

PEOPLE PROBLEMS

▶ Your lack of training
▶ Your own unhappiness
▶ Disillusionment with the job
▶ Personality conflict
▶ Unhealthy competition
▶ Customer conflict
▶ Ineffective team
▶ Factions within team, department, or corporation
▶ Discrimination

65

Organizational Problems.

Your boss tells you to do one thing. Your supervisor expects something else. And you're caught in the middle of an organizational problem. Tracy joined the art department of a middle-sized graphic arts company. She was hired to speed up production so that her department would meet deadlines. But Tracy soon discovered the department's problems ran deeper than she'd anticipated.

"I was told to increase production and speed it up. But the artists already worked overtime—and as fast as I've ever seen artists work. I needed to hire more artists to get the job done, but I couldn't get the firm to listen. The week I got there, two more artists quit and I wasn't given authority to replace them." People weren't the problem; the organization was. The organizational problem made it impossible for Tracy to succeed unless the company admitted the real problem.

Organizational problems arise when the chain of command is unclear.

F A C T O I D :
A flowchart is a diagram of a corporation's hierarchy of authority or a chart showing steps in a sequence of operations.

Other organizational problems arise when the chain of command is unclear. Employees get caught in the middle of power struggles and everybody suffers. If the problem isn't correctly identified, people get blamed.

Unpredictable changes in the marketplace or the economy can cause downsizing. You may not have the necessary power to fix organizational problems, but recognizing them can help you find your way through the maze.

ORGANIZATIONAL PROBLEMS

▶ Inability to get the resources you need to do the task
▶ Unclear chain of command
▶ Changes in the economy
▶ Changes in the marketplace
▶ Overlapping responsibilities

Mechanical Problems

The third kind of problem is the mechanical or technical problem. If your hard drive crashes or your modem won't work, you look for a technical solution. The more you know about computers, the better. If you know you'll need to use projectors, copiers, or machinery, do all you can to become an expert.

Other mechanical problems come from telephones, inadequate phone service, telecommunication breakdowns, fax machines, and problems on the Internet.

MECHANICAL PROBLEMS	
Computers	Telecommunications equipment
Telephones	Phone service
Fax	Assembly-line machines
Copiers	Voice mail

MANY-SIDED PROBLEMS

Since most problems are complex, you have to examine them from every angle. Arnette was head of the yearbook staff her senior year in high school. The problem was that yearbook sales had been so low the past three years, her principal threatened to cut yearbook funds drastically.

Arnette had a problem. Why were sales so bad? She needed to examine the problem from all possible angles. She and her committee considered the quality, price, timing, and advertising of the yearbooks. They analyzed the audience and discovered that almost all seniors bought a copy, but nobody else did. They put together a survey to find out why. They discovered that underclassmen didn't buy the yearbook because they didn't expect to see many photos of their class. And Arnette's committee had the focus they needed. They took lots of photos of each class and made sure students could expect to see them in the new yearbook. Yearbook sales nearly doubled.

After graduating from college, Arnette took a job in hotel management in Hawaii. When the hotel ran into a similar problem, Arnette remembered her yearbook success.

"The hotel was losing money. But our ads in vacation magazines had paid off. All our target audience—mainland vacationers—responded and booked holidays. We analyzed the problem and came up with the lack of specialty bookings. We expanded the audience to golfers, honeymooners, just as I'd expanded to underclassmen in high school."

THE SIX Ws

One method of analysis to identify the real problem is using the six W questions: who, what, when, where, why and what if.

For example, imagine that your company has been producing the most adorable widget for the cheapest price, but nobody's buying. Ask *who*. Who are these people that should be buying? Analyze your audience. Run a demographic study. Put together a survey.

Ask *what.* What applies to the quality of your product. Hmmm. When you check that out, you discover that your widgets, adorable as they may be, fall apart the first day. You have a quality problem.

You still ask *when.* Are you advertising and selling at the best times? Yes. Ask *where?* Are you reaching the right locales for your product, putting them on the right shelf in the right stores? Yep. Ask *why.* Why do you charge what you charge? Why produce the number you do? No problem there. Ask *what if.* What if you stopped producing widgets, switched to a new product, made them larger or smaller or in different colors? No, that's not it.

And so you're back to quality. Now, all you have to do is figure a way to increase the quality without increasing the cost. You might cut costs somewhere else (delivery costs, advertising, etc.). But at least you have the problem clearly defined and can move ahead with the solution.

THE SWOT TEST

Another way to look at a situation in order to zero in on the real problem is to run the SWOT test: strengths, weaknesses, opportunities, seasonal threats.

Take the failing widgets. What are its strengths? They're so adorable! And they're cheap. What are the weaknesses? Widgets fall apart. What opportunities are you missing for sales? Ads, testimonials, shelf space, variety of colors? Are there any seasonal threats? Do they do well or poorly at Christmas? Do sales drop dramatically in summer?

ANALYZING THE PROBLEM

The Six Ws	The SWOT Test
Who? (audience)	Strengths
What? (quality)	Weaknesses
When? (timing)	Opportunities
Where? (locale)	Threats—seasonal
Why?	Cost, number, etc
What if?	Possibilities

BE INFORMED

The only way to find the answers to your specific questions is to do your homework. Research the problem. Several years ago the Red Cross began to run low on blood supplies. The obvious solution was to send out more pleas for donors. But a problem-solving team took the time to analyze the problem.

Why was there a shortage of blood? It wasn't an increased need for blood. The number of volunteer donors had plummeted. They surveyed would-be donors to more clearly define the problem. That's when they learned the real problem. Fear of AIDS. People knew just enough about AIDS to fear blood and needles. No amount of pleading was going to change their minds. A campaign to inform and inspire donors was undertaken.

You know the pains and rewards of research if you've ever written a research paper. If you skimmed over secondary sources and ignored the best information available, you probably omitted key arguments and data. And your grade reflected your laziness. But students are not the only ones who can stop too soon in their information-gathering and end up with false conclusions. In October 1967, the Soviet Union launched a space probe designed to crash on the surface of Venus and send back information about temperature and conditions on the planet. When the space probe stopped transmitting, it was presumed the craft had hit its target. The data sent at that point indicated temperature and atmospheric pressure that could possibly sustain life as we know it!

But there was a problem that wasn't discovered until much later. The Russian craft had malfunctioned and stopped transmitting signals when it was still 15 miles from the surface of Venus. Actually, the Venus temperatures turned out to be 75 to 100 times that of Earth, too hot for life as we know it. Keep going until you get to the bottom of the problem.

Stick with the problem until you're sure you've correctly identified and defined it.

Before we leave this chapter, here's a promise and a warning. Stick with the problem until you're sure you've correctly identified and defined it. Persistence pays off. But be careful what you set your mind on. Ask the right questions. If your question is, "Why am I so stupid?" or, "Why did I mess up?" your mind will keep focusing on your faults, destructively dissecting your weaknesses. Instead, focus on the problem at hand. Keep going until you can see through to a solution.

The world cares very little about what a man or woman knows. It is what the man or woman is able to do that counts.

—Booker T. Washington

EXERCISE

1. Clearly define three real problems facing you right now. Next to each, indicate if it's a people, mechanical, or organizational problem—or a combination.

2. What can you do with your remaining time in school to head off potential mechanical problems in your career?

3. What kinds of people problems (including *you*) do you run into most often?

6

C H A P T E R   S I X

STEP 2: DEFINE GOALS AND OBJECTIVES

Before you begin to establish goals and objectives and go forward on the solution to your problem, double-check to be sure you've properly identified the problem. Sort out the cause from the effect. If you don't, your solution is bound to be incomplete.

For example, your English grade has fallen this semester. True, that's a problem. But it's an effect. And as you set your goal for the rest of the semester and determine to raise your grade, you need to explore the cause. You've always gotten A's in English, so you're not stupid. You've done your homework and done okay on tests. What's left? Class participation. You've been sleeping in class lately. Could that be it?

You're closer to the cause. Your goals are not only going to include raising your grade. You're going to plan to stay awake in class. But keep going. Sleeping in class is an effect, too. You never fell asleep in class until this semester. What's changed in your life to cause you to sleep in English class?

Then you get it. You've been staying up late every night to watch *Twilight Zone* reruns. Your goals and objectives will have to start there, maybe limiting the *Zone* to Friday nights.

CONNECTING GOALS TO
THE REAL PROBLEM

The problem's definition should include its cause and effect. And everything should connect to your goals. "My late-night *Twilight Zone* viewing is causing me to sleep in class and get a lower grade in English." Then you're ready to set goals that will speak to the real problem.

In the business world, it's important to define the problem in terms of the company's goals, in light of their overall purpose. "What caused the effect?" instead of "Whose fault is it?" "Aaron's poor relationship with his team is causing the team to fall short of January production goals."

SETTING GOALS

You set goals all the time. Remember your New Year's resolutions? (Probably not if you're out of January.) Those were goals: "This year I will lose weight." "This year I'm going to save money...be nicer to my parents...get a job." Goals are the way you want things to look, the end product.

Business goals aren't that much different from personal goals. "This year we'll improve our corporate image." "This year we'll land new accounts from big investors." "This year we'll increase profits and cut costs."

A goal is an end one strives to attain. The clearer your vision of the end, the better shot you have of reaching it.

Goals define our mission in life. Without goals we have no direction, and without direction, we have no criteria to judge....

**—Amy Lindgren,
president of Prototype Career Services**

VISUALIZATION

Visualization is the practice of envisioning, or holding a mental picture. Visualizing your goal means you picture what things will look like when you've achieved your goal.

Barry, now a successful sales manager, says he learned the art of visualization from his high school

(Courtesy: Daren M. Alix)

Whether it's sinking a foul shot or delivering a presentation, visualizing your goal can help you to accomplish it.

basketball coach. "I had problems with my foul shot. So Coach had me stand at the line, get set for the shot then try to picture myself shooting the ball and catching nothing but net. We did it in practice. Then right before I took a foul shot in a game, I always visualized the ball going in."

When Barry joined his sales team, he applied his visualization technique. "The first time I had to give a big presentation, I was really nervous. So I kept picturing myself standing up, pointing at the graphs and being at ease and great. It helped."

Visualization is more than just a mental trick. If you can't see clearly to the end of the line, chances are your goal lacks clarity.

DOS AND DON'TS
OF SETTING GOALS

Do	Don't
Get to the root cause.	Settle for the effect.
Be specific.	Be general.
Relate goal to overall purpose.	Be uninformed.
Include a time frame.	Make a wish and hope.
Visualize the end.	Lump goals and objectives together.

GOOD GOALS

Talking about goals can get confusing. We can talk about long-range goals and short-range goals. A desire to be a forest ranger when you grow up could be considered a long-range goal. Your desire to make the soccer team next month is a relatively short-term goal.

Good goals are specific and definable.

Your company may have a general, humanitarian goal of serving the community or fostering understanding. But the goals you'll be dealing with directly are much more focused. Good goals are specific and definable. Otherwise, you'll never know if you reach them.

For example, let's go back to your New Year's resolutions. If your goal is to lose weight or look good, how will you know for sure when you've arrived? Have you completed your goal as soon as you lose one ounce? If you lose 50 pounds, who's to say you look good?

Most businesses would share the goal of increasing profits. But the widget manufacturer will have a more useful goal if it's specific: "Maintain overhead costs at current level, but increase the sale of widgets by 10%." Now they can visualize the end—more widgets, more profit.

80

GET REAL

For a goal to be good and workable, or helpful, it has to be specific. It also needs to be realistic. What happens to your New Year's resolutions when you set your goals too high? You set a goal to lose 60 pounds and date the most popular senior in high school. (Fat chance.) Chances are you'll get discouraged early because you know there's no way to reach that goal. And even if you lose 20 pounds and have a decent date for homecoming, you're still not satisfied.

Goals must be attainable. Companies have to do research before they set their goals. They can't just wish a figure and hope for the best. Go ahead and dream the impossible dream. But when you write down your goals, get real.

SETTING OBJECTIVES

In most cases, objectives are bite-sized, measurable goals, that if completed will lead to the fulfillment of an overall goal. Say you decide your goal is to lose 10 pounds by June 1, the date the swimming pool opens. You've made your goal specific and measurable, and given yourself a time frame. Good.

Now, it's time to break that goal up into chunks. That's setting objectives. Each objective should be

Objectives are bite-sized, measurable goals.

measurable, so you'll know if you've reached it. You figure it out and settle on a half-pound a week. You'll

OBJECTIVES FOR WRITING AN "A" TERM PAPER

Goal: To research, write and turn in an "A" term paper by due date, March 16.

Objective: Brainstorm 20 topics and select one by February 1.

Objective: To draft thesis by February 3.

Objective: Complete general library research by February 10.

Objective: Outline completed by February 15.

Objective: Specific research completed by February 25.

Objective: Write the first draft of paper by March 1.

Objective: Write the second draft by March 7.

Objective: Final draft typed and proofed by March 14.

weigh yourself weekly and keep a record in a little book by the scale. Now, how are you going to accomplish this goal?

First, you will exercise 5 days a week for 30 minutes a time. Next, you need to change your eating habits. You make an objective to read three cookbooks on low-fat recipes. You'll pack your lunch and make your own dinners and breakfasts. You continue with your objectives until you're confident that fulfilling each objective will lead you to your goal. By the time you pull on that swimsuit, you'll be 10 pounds thinner.

You may have to research each objective. Will losing a half-pound a week bring you to your goal? What does it take in exercise to lose weight? What kinds of exercise are best?

Good objectives usually combine a measurable end with an action and a time frame. They relate directly to the overall goal. It's like a set of footprints leading to a treasure. If someone follows each step, he should end up at the treasure. If a step is missing, or the steps begin to veer away from the treasure, he won't get there. All you have to do to reach your goal is to reach each objective along the way.

But how do you reach those objectives? Read on.

EXERCISE

GOOD GOALS!

1. Which of the following goals is specific? Can you alter the general goals to make them more specific?

    a. Our company will improve its corporate image.

    b. I'll get Tom to take me to a movie by the end of this month.

    c. Our department will increase sales by 10% this year.

    d. The company will downsize its personnel 25%, with no more than 10% loss in productivity.

    e. This year I'll become popular.

2. Now, choose one of the above specific goals you've created and list at least five objectives under it.

7
STEP 3: GENERATE SOLUTIONS

You've identified and defined the problem. You've drawn up specific goals and objectives. Now you need to decide how to meet those objectives. Take that term paper you scheduled in the last chapter. Goals and objectives are in place. You have time limits and measurable outcomes.

But what will you write about? Now it's time to generate ideas. Lots of ideas. The more choices you give yourself—the more possible solutions—the better your final selection will be.

Want to write on dinosaurs? Your paper will be boring, like nearly everybody else's, if you choose the first idea that comes to you. Instead, think of 10, 20, 50 possible topics so you end up with a winner: "The Stegosaurus in All of Us."

Nature operates by profusion. Think of the nearly infinite number of seeds that fall to earth, only a fraction of which take root to become trees;...of the millions of sperm competing so fiercely to fertilize one small egg. Similarly, human beings engaged in the creative process explore an astronomical number of possible patterns before settling on an idea.

—Gabriele Lusser Rico, *Writing the Natural Way*

MULTIPLE CHOICES

Are you one of those people who never feels creative? Not the creative type. You lack originality. Creativity and originality are essentials for any problem solver, and your employer will expect you to bring a degree of creativity to your work.

Don't panic. Creativity is within your reach if you're willing to practice coming up with multiple choices. Learn to generate lots of ideas.

Not long ago, *TEEN Magazine* decided to change its image. They wanted to reach the more subtle, mature, older teens. When goals and objectives were set, the magazine hired public relations consultants to come up with possible ways the magazine might change its image.

Chris Bliss, part of the public relations team, explains what happened next. "We met as a team to come up with ideas. It was rather like a game show, where contestants had to spout off as many words or phrases as they could think of in five minutes."

They listed possible changes, such as lipstick and lipstick colors, tone of writing, color of cover, models for cover, inside art, features, headings and graphics, products advertised and so on. "At the end of five minutes, the four of us had about 120 ideas. We had a lot to choose from."

That's what you want at this stage of problem solving. Multiple choices. So, how do you get them? Brainstorm.

DOS AND DON'TS
OF BRAINSTORMING SESSIONS

Do	Don't
Speak/write fast.	Think.
Say the first thing that comes to mind.	Censure yourself.
Be vulnerable.	Analyze.
Respect every idea.	Slow down.

BRAINSTORMING

Brainstorming is the practice of quickly generating multiple ideas, without restraining the free flow of possible solutions. Katie brainstormed her way through high school and college and straight onto a team of researchers in the Southwest. She explains, "In high school, brainstorming was how we raised money for projects, came up with group ideas, decided on a science fair project. I brainstormed big assignments so I'd have several ideas in case one didn't work out. It's the same technique we use where I work to solve every problem we run into."

Remember the discussion in chapter 2 of right brain/left brain thinking? In a way, your right brain holds the inspired ideas, those crazy notions that just might be what your work team is looking for. But your left brain, rational and logical, realizes how bizarre the right brain ideas can get. So good, reliable left brain jumps in and censors that bright idea before it comes out.

Does it confirm what you've always suspected—that you do have a split personality? Not really. You just have two distinct kinds of thinking going on at the same time.

Brainstorming is designed to get those great, sometimes hidden, ideas out before you squelch them. In order for the process to work, you need to follow a few ground rules.

Set a Time Limit

If you're brainstorming a topic for your term paper or an invention to make you a millionaire, you'll have better luck brainstorming ideas for five focused minutes than you will trying to come up with something for five hours. Set a time limit. Get out all the right-brain ideas as fast as you can. After a few minutes, your left brain will step in and take over anyway.

When you're in a group brainstorming session, your team might want to set a time limit—say, 10 minutes—for pure brainstorming. Then you can step back and see what you've come up with.

No Judgments Here

If it's so hard to get these fresh, original (and sometimes bizarre) ideas out to ourselves, imagine working at problem solving with a team. Each member of your work team needs to abide by this ground rule: no judgments during brainstorming.

If a team member feels his ideas are going to be evaluated as soon as he says them, that's the end of his contribution to the brainstorming session. He will

Ground rule: no judgments during brainstorming.

89

censure himself before anyone else gets a chance. And that censured solution may be the one you need.

Trust has to exist in a team brainstorming session, or the best solutions may be stifled before they leave that right brain.

Every Idea Has Merit

After all the ideas are out, the team should generate a long list of possible solutions. Every idea is worth recording.

It's time to see what you've come up with. Instead of heading straight for the two or three ideas that sound the best, a great problem solver will keep this rule in mind: Every idea has merit. Great problem solvers look at every idea, no matter how bizarre. Some of the best solutions come as a result of piecing together bits of several seemingly implausible solutions.

Imagine your problem is that you're failing history. Your goal is to get a B by the end of the semester. You put together objectives and a time frame. Now you brainstorm, following all the ground rules.

First, you turn off the CD player and TV and lock your door. Desk cleared, you sit with paper and pen ready to write down every possible solution that comes to you for getting a B in history. Go!

90

- Cheat.
- Meet with teacher.
- Study with X.
- Ask Mom for help.
- Go to counseling.
- Read outside books.
- Ask for extra credit.
- Study my old tests.
- Get a tutor.
- Beg teacher for a B.
- Study with Y or Z.
- Ask Dad for help.
- Transfer.
- Study one hour a night.
- Find last year's final.
- Take speed reading.

When five minutes are up, put your pen down. At first glance, you've come up with some pretty stupid ideas. But, you've vowed to consider every idea. You can't cheat and copy Smart Sally's test. But you could call Sally and ask if you could look at her last five quizzes so you could correct your paper and have the right answers to study for the final.

You know it won't do any good to beg your teacher to please give you a B. But you might ask what you need to do in order to bring your grade up to a B.

Brainstorming can help you with problems ranging from a topic for your term paper, a gift for your boyfriend, a place to take your girlfriend—to what your employer should do to increase profits. Practice the art of brainstorming. The ability to come up with multiple solutions will give you a reputation as a problem solver.

TECHNIQUES OF BRAINSTORMING

Sitting at your desk and jotting down ideas as fast as you can is one way of brainstorming—*listing*. Working with a team of problem solvers and calling out ideas as they come to you is another method. Many other techniques of brainstorming can be used to unleash right-brain thoughts before the left brain has a chance to censor them.

Some of these methods will work for you; others won't. Use them as tools and store the techniques in your mental toolbox, a bag of tricks you can pull out when you need them to help you fix problems.

Word Association

You've heard about word associations used by psychiatrists. You've probably played a game built on word associations. "When I say a word, give me the first word that comes into your mind. *Love.*" Your uninhibited answer will tell a lot about you. "Bruno." "Puppy." "Fear." "Sex." "Impossible." If your answer surprises even you, then your right brain slipped one past the more orderly left brain. And that's the idea.

How can this help you solve a problem at work? Imagine that your boss wants your work team to come up with a new motto, a slogan for your product, a cleanser called "Green Clean." One way to generate ideas would be to take each word in the product name and apply word association: "What's the first thing that comes into your mind when I say *green*?"

"Spring." "Pasture." "Lime." "New." "Inexperienced."

You do the same kind of word association with "Clean." Then see if you've come up with a potential motto: "Use Green Clean and bring springtime to your house."

Clustering or Mapping

Clustering, like free-word association, is a brainstorming technique to help you spill out flashes of inspiration in unplanned relationships. Thoughts come out as clusters.

In clustering, you write a trigger word in the center of your paper. Circle the word. Then, as fast as you can, write the words or ideas that pop into your head. Circle each word and connect word balloons that come together. When that thought process slows, start another chain of word balloons.

93

This cluster of ideas focused on possible directions for an ad agency to take on a Christmas campaign:

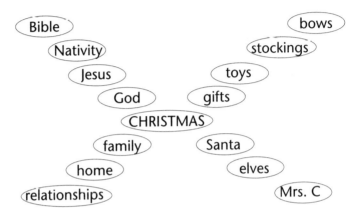

When you finish the cluster, look it over carefully—not just for words, but for the clusters, the relationship between words. You may have released a complex design or connection you can put to good use.

Freewriting

Your English teacher may have introduced you to freewriting. "Class, everybody write whatever comes into your mind for five minutes." That's a dangerous offer. But it can also be an effective brainstorming technique if your mind is stuck on a problem.

Cari wrestled with a customer service problem the first year she worked for an international airlines. She explains how freewriting helped her come up with a needed solution. "It was the first time a customer had complained that I wasn't helpful. Her problem was she didn't have the frequent-flyer mileage to get the prize she wanted. That's what I told her, but she wanted more."

Cari took five minutes away from phones, while the customer talked to her supervisor. "I just started writing the first thing that came into my head—that the woman was a nutcase, I hated my job. Then I started writing her possibilities. She could get a partial ticket to St. Louis, have the mileage she needed and get her upgrade on that."

Cari quickly jotted down the solution and passed it to her supervisor. Her quick thinking didn't go unnoticed. An account of that incident went into her folder and helped get her high marks on her first evaluation.

Freewriting can be freewheeling, or it can be guided. Cari might have started out by focusing on the customer's options. Both methods can help bring your best ideas to the surface.

Now that you're loaded with possible solutions, it's time for a plan of action.

EXERCISE

1. Give yourself five minutes to brainstorm as many solutions as possible for the following situations:

   a. It's time to turn in your three-page test, but you're out of staples. How can you get the pages to stay together?

   b. Your new concoction, Orange Delight soda, isn't selling well at your school. How can you get students at your school to spend their money on Orange Delight instead of Coke and Pepsi?

2. Try clustering the following words and see what you come out with:

   success

   failure

   hate

   friendship

8 CHAPTER EIGHT
STEP 4: MAKE A PLAN OF ACTION

If you're following these simple problem-solving steps, you should have a bunch of possible solutions to your problem. Now, all you have to do is decide which solution is the pick of the litter.

EVALUATING CHOICES

Remember how important it was in the last step to hold off judgment. You didn't want to hamper the free flow of ideas and possibilities. You kept that analytical, critical side of yourself leashed, held at bay...for this very moment.

It's time to analyze your choices and formulate an action plan. If the last chapter celebrated the powers of right-brain thinking, this chapter testifies to your need for all the logical powers residing in your left brain.

When Brad started working for a solar panel company in Hawaii, he thought he'd reached his dream job. And what job could be more secure than selling solar panels in a location with so much sun!

But right away Brad saw he was wrong. His company was in danger of going under. He had been hired in hopes he might shine a new perspective on his team's problem. His boss handed Brad a file of possible solutions they had considered. Did they need a better product? Better salespeople? A new location? More advertising? What could they do to attract enough customers?

Brad studied the data gathered on every conceivable answer. His team already had determined the root problem. They had a great product, super location, experienced salespeople, and a hefty advertising budget. The problem was the way Hawaiians viewed solar panel companies in general. Most companies had fly-by-night reputations.

Brad was closer to a solution, but he still had choices to evaluate. The team brainstormed more possible ideas for establishing the company's positive image.

As Brad evaluated their choices, he narrowed the possibilities to two:

1. Conduct an ad campaign to convince people their company was not one of the fly-by-nighters.

2. Make a positive image for the company through an all new campaign.

In evaluating these final options, Brad gathered more information, data, statistics. He interviewed potential customers. He studied what other, similar companies had done and what had failed. At last, Brad was ready with his recommendation for an action plan.

MODIFY AND SELECT A PLAN OF ACTION

Use your powers of analytical thought to evaluate each possible solution. Investigate rigorously. But the time will come to make up your mind. You may modify one solution, combine two or more possible solutions, but you need to settle on one plan of action.

Brad's final recommendation for his solar panel company was to begin a vigorous, positive, all new ad campaign. Trying to explain themselves to the public would only link them with fly-by-night outfits. Brad suggested they proceed as if people believed in them. Brad drew up a plan of action.

LIST STEPS IN YOUR PLAN OF ACTION

Once the solution is settled on, everybody sets to work on detailing the plan. Here's where you need your skills at setting goals and objectives. Break down the larger goal (change our image by next year) into smaller goals and objectives.

As soon as Brad and his solar panel company settled on their plan of action—to conduct an island-wide positive image campaign over the next 12 months—they got down to business. A step-by-step strategy targeted all local media. Their own materials and flyers were rewritten. Salespeople were called in for seminars on projecting confidence and the right image.

Over the next year, Brad developed ads by "the Sunshine Guys." They had their own jingle, their own success stories, their own emblem. Eventually, the whole island could sing that jingle and grew to trust the Sunshine Guys. The bold plan of action had set Brad's company apart from their competitors.

A PLAN OF ACTION INCLUDES...

▶ A clear statement of the overall plan

▶ Goals and clear-cut objectives

▶ A step-by-step strategy

▶ A schedule, with deadlines

▶ Allocation of human and financial resources

▶ Delegation of jobs

▶ Contingency plans

▶ An internal review system

SCHEDULING

A timeline of action is an integral part of forming a plan of action. When will new brochures need to be issued? March 15? Then that means the rewritten copy must be completed by...which means the writer or publicity firm must be hired by.... Scheduling needs to be specific, realistic, encompassing every part of the action plan.

Each objective should have its own deadline or deadlines. And those deadlines have to be coordinated with all other objectives. In Brad's Hawaiian campaign, they decided on a blitz, with print, radio, and television media starting the same day.

If a number of individuals have to be contacted, is the order important? If so, schedule accordingly.

One of the worst crimes a team member can commit against his team is to miss a deadline. Don't do it. Your geography teacher may have been understanding of missed deadlines. She granted you an extension. But your team can't afford this luxury. If you fail to meet your deadline, you could single-handedly derail your company's action plan.

If you fail to meet your deadline, you could single-handedly derail your company's action plan.

DELEGATING

Once all the individual parts of the plan of action have been detailed, goals and objectives in place, a time-

(V. Harlow/Russell Library)

Individuals working as a team can achieve their goals more efficiently when each one is assigned the tasks for which they are best suited.

line established, it's time to settle who does what. A good manager or team leader will delegate wisely. Work should be as evenly distributed as possible. And team members should be working in areas of their strengths.

_____

I not only use all the brains I have, but all I can borrow.

—President Woodrow Wilson

As the rookie on the problem-solving team, you may not get the jobs you want. The team may put you in charge of copying materials, when all you want is a crack at television ads. Realize that you're going to have to earn those glitzier jobs. Give all you've got to whatever assignments you are given. Then you may do better next time.

If you get to volunteer for tasks, don't just ask for the more glamorous or the easier jobs. Everybody will know why your hand went up, and they won't appreciate it. Instead, volunteer for tasks you know you can do well. Communicate. Ask what's involved, and be honest about your strengths and weaknesses. Ask for the legwork jobs nobody wants. Do more than you have to do just to hold up your end.

Volunteer for tasks you know you can do well.

Don't consider your job done when you've accomplished everything you've been delegated. You're not done until the whole plan is accomplished. So, if you find yourself with free time on your hands, ask your teammates what you can do to help them with their responsibilities.

PUTTING IT ALL TOGETHER

A sound action plan includes other essentials, too. How much money will you need to see the plan through? Where will you get the funds? Will you need more personnel? More space? More direction?

The way to achieve success is first to have a defi-nite, clear, practical idea—a goal, an objective. Second, have the necessary means to achieve your ends—wisdom, money, materials, methods. Third, adjust all your means to that end.

—Aristotle

Every great Plan A has a good Plan B waiting in the wings just in case. Chapter 9 deals with contingency plans and troubleshooting.

EXERCISE

Draw up your own plan of action for successfully completing the best double date ever.

1. Brainstorm your possibilities. (Who and where.)
2. Evaluate your choices. (She's cool, but would hang up on me. He's great, but he's too old for me. Wrestling would be nice, but too expensive.)
3. Modify and select a plan. (State it clearly in writing.)
4. List the steps you'll need to pull off your plan. (Invitations, transportation, etc.)
5. Schedule the above steps. (Give yourself a deadline for making that phone call.)
6. Delegate. (If you're still double-dating, divide the work.)
7. Put it together. (Go ahead and do it.)

CHAPTER NINE
9 STEP 5: FOLLOW THROUGH

You've done it! You've gone from a brainstorming session of wild ideas, through research and analysis, to come up with a plan of action. You've broken that plan into detailed steps with deadlines. Assignments have been delegated, and your team is ready to charge!

But hold on just a minute. Don't forget about the follow-through step. The best time to begin follow through is *before* you start.

ANTICIPATION SAVES ON FRUSTRATION

Before you race out of the conference room and head separate ways, anticipate potential problems with your plan. Try a variation on a brainstorming session. Ask, "What could possibly go wrong?"

Humans don't always react the way you think they will. If your plan hinges on certain people, ask *what if...* "What if she's too angry to say yes?" "What if he won't see us?" "What if her schedule is too full, or she doesn't like the plan?"

Money never goes quite as far as you think it will. What if you run out of money in your ad campaign? Could the radio have raised its commercial rate? And what if you get into the campaign and see it's not working?

Should you ask for more help, just in case? Do you have enough access to the copy machine to...? And what if the city has another blackout! Anticipate.

No amount of planning can predict everything. As analytical and logical as our left brain may be, it's not omniscient. But if we can anticipate what might go wrong, we'll be better prepared and hopefully less frustrated.

Jerry works for a large trucking company, supplying rigs to clients. He does all he can to anticipate possible problems for his customers. "Anticipating trouble is the easiest part of my job. I helped raise my six younger brothers and sisters. Something was always bound to go wrong." He explains that he feels it's part of his duty to prepare his customers for unforeseen trouble. "I check the weather and try to let them know if that might slow delivery. I always tell them somebody might return the rig late to us, or it might need repair. Then if something happens, they remember I warned them. And they're not quite so crazy."

CONTINGENCIES

A contingency is something that depends on unforeseen or accidental occurrences. You do all you can to make sure your plan of action will succeed. But just in case, it's a good idea to plan for any contingency. If your Plan A falls apart, do you have a Plan B?

If you worked through the problem-solving process, you do have contingency plans. When you generated all those possible solutions and evaluated their worth, you left behind several alternative plans. So, before you start Plan A, make sure you select a Plan B to keep on the back burner. Hopefully, you'll never need it. But if you do, you'll be glad it's there waiting for you.

If your Plan A falls apart, do you have a Plan B?

Tess directed a nursing home in a major city. Although they were in a densely populated area, the number of patients sagged and so did funds. The administrative team decided to raise money and at the same time get neighborhood residents in for a visit. If residents could see for themselves how nice the rooms were inside, the staff believed the problem would be solved.

Tess and her staff planned to hold a community rummage and yard sale at the nursing home. They'd raise a little cash. But more importantly, neighbors could have the chance to check out the nursing home.

All went according to well-thought-out plans, except for one unforeseen problem. Neighbors poured into the yard sale, but nobody ventured inside the nursing home. But Tess remembered one of the plans they had rejected in favor of the yard sale. One of the staff members had suggested a craft and quilt show.

Tess grabbed the quilts off the yard tables and hung them *inside* the nursing home. Now visitors *had* to go inside to view the quilts. Once inside, many neighbors took a tour of the home. Tess was grateful for the contingency plan.

TROUBLESHOOTING

Good working teams try to troubleshoot problems before they happen.

Troubleshooting means investigating, finding and wiping out the source of trouble. Most troubleshooting occurs when the plan runs into real problems. But good working teams try to troubleshoot problems *before* they happen.

How can you troubleshoot a problem ahead of time? Take a test run. Try your strategy on a small, representative audience. Jay Leno has a habit of trying out his jokes and monologue material at a small night-club before delivering them on the *Tonight Show.* If the joke bombs in the test audience, he may have

108

saved himself a big embarrassment on national television. He can "fix" the joke, or throw it out altogether.

If at all possible, try your plan out first, before you commit all the troops. Then alter the plan before it's too late.

FLEXIBILITY

Anticipate potential problems. Make contingency plans. Troubleshoot your idea. But no matter how thorough you are, you'll run into problems. Be willing to flex.

Flexibility is highly valued in a problem solver. Why? Because even top dollar can't buy omniscience. Movie advertisers put together a short film clip, or trailer, to promote movies. The clip includes quick scenes or snatches of dialogue from the actual movie, a slogan or catchphrase ("Be afraid. Be very afraid.") or staged testimonials ("I was so scared, I spilled my popcorn!").

But as much money as producers put into these trailers, the ad people can miss the mark. So they have to be flexible. If marketing surveys come back that no one is buying this future film as a scary movie, they pick a different clip, call it the greatest love story ever told, and run a new trailer.

You may not have the resources to put together a whole new campaign. But you owe your employer

109

and your coworkers flexibility. When you run into a brick wall, you can crumble into pieces, or you can flex and find a way around it.

PERSISTENCE

Remember, we're talking about solving a problem, a real problem. Your job as a problem solver isn't finished when you get your grand action plan. Your job isn't over until that problem is solved.

Each person on your team should persist in the completion of every objective. If some director won't talk to you on the phone, show up in person. If that doesn't work, send a telegram, flowers, or a chocolate chip cookie. Persist. Don't stop until you get what you want.

Keep in mind that vision of the end. Remember why you started in the first place. It takes persistence to stay with a plan until it's completed.

Some men give up their designs when they have almost reached the goal; while others, on the contrary, obtain a victory by exerting, at the last moment, more vigorous efforts than before.

—Polybius

CELEBRATE

Working out and following through with your plan can be stressful. Take time out to celebrate each victory.

▶ When someone pulls off her part of the plan, everybody should join in the celebration and success.

▶ Mark the milestones with a celebration. Make sure you get together regularly for progress reports. When you reach your first week and everybody's right on schedule, pat yourselves on the back. Encourage each other and keep the end in plain sight.

▶ When you get any positive feedback on your plan, celebrate. The celebration might take the form of a presentation, illustrating the amazing effect of your master plan in action.

▶ Finally, when you've made it to the end and the problem is solved, don't forget to celebrate. Too often, that's when the team adjourns. Then the moment of shared triumph is over, and the team has missed an opportunity to deepen team unity.

Never one thing and seldom one person can make for a success. It takes a number of them merging into one perfect whole.
—Marie Dressler

111

FOLLOW THROUGH
WITH CELEBRATION

- At one-week point

- At one-month point

- With every
  individual success

- At positive feedback
  on the plan

- When an objective is
  reached

- When you arrive
  at the end

- When you overcome
  an obstacle

- Before moving on

When the students at a West Coast school spear-
headed the local United Way drive, they took advan-
tage of every opportunity to celebrate victories. All
over the city, students set out thermometer signs,
clearly marked with eight lines, each indicating a dollar amount. As contributions came in, students
painted the thermometer in red to show how much
money had been raised and how far they hoped to
go. And whenever a school or business reached a new

level, students celebrated. They showed up personally and congratulated participants.

Don't miss the chance to celebrate success.

LEARNING FROM MISTAKES

Finally, the best way to grow as a problem solver is to learn from mistakes. You can learn from your own mistakes, those of others, or the mistakes of your company as a whole. Keep a notebook or a file of what you learn. Your experiences can do more for you than...say...a whole book on problem solving. But only if you learn from your mistakes.

_____

There are three classes of people in the world. The first learn from their own experience—these are wise; the second learn from the experience of others—these are happy; the third neither learn from their own experiences nor the experiences of others—these are fools.

—Philip Chesterfield

113

EXERCISE

1. Name three mistakes you've made in the past three years, and explain what you've learned from each mistake.

2. What kinds of contingency plans do sports teams need?

3. Make a New Year's resolution. Now, imagine everything that might go wrong. What might you do to reduce the risk of failure?

10 CHAPTER TEN
NO PROBLEM

DECISION MAKING

Still hate decisions? Do you only buy one brand of cereal because you can't stand making decisions early in the morning? Well, now that you have a method for solving problems, you also have a decision-making method. With a few minor adjustments, you can use the same steps to arrive at most any decision.

In life, never spend more than 10% of your time on the problem, and spend at least 90% of your time on the solution.
—fundamental rule of business

Let's see how the same, basic five-step approach works for making personal decisions. Suppose you have enough money saved to buy your first car. What are you going to choose?

STEP 1. IDENTIFY AND DEFINE THE DECISION TO BE MADE

You stand on the threshold of your first car purchase. But to identify this necessary decision, you may have come through a lot. Your questioning may have started with, "Should I take the bus or call my buddy?" "Should I walk or go back to bed?"

But you've sorted through the pile of questions and are determined to buy a car—some car, any car. Obviously, the decision is which car you should buy.

Or is it?

A good problem solver makes unpopular decisions when necessary, but considers the impact of decisions, remaining sensitive to other departments and individuals.
—Employee Appraiser

STEP 2. WEIGH GOALS AND OBJECTIVES

As a business needs to relate its short-range goals to its long-term goals, or mission statement, you need to base your decision on your long-range goals, too. Check your short-term decisions against your long-term goals.

Your long-range goal may be to go to college. If you need this car money for your first year's tuition, you have another decision to make.

But, we'll say you're not threatening your college career with the purchase. So you define the decision to be made: Which car shall I buy?

STEP 3. GENERATE CHOICES

Now you do your homework—your car-buyer's homework, that is. You go through car showrooms, school parking lots, want ads. You list every possible car for sale in the United States and beyond.

The sky's the limit in your dream list. Leave that Porsche and Ferrari right where they are, at the top of the list. Keep going. Ask Uncle Chuck for the name of his truck. Are they still selling station wagons?

Remember, this is the brainstorming phase. No censuring allowed.

FIVE FOES OF DECISION MAKING
1. Fear of failure
2. Rush to judgment
3. Laziness
4. Short-sighted disregard for long-range goals
5. Self-deception

STEP 4. EVALUATE YOUR CHOICES

Now it's time to get real. Evaluate your choices according to your needs and ability. (You can still get the color you want.) The more information the better here. Try *Consumer Reports,* the Internet, car owners, a good mechanic.

FACTOID:

Intelligence is derived from two words—
inter (meaning "between") and legere (meaning "to choose"). An intelligent person is one who learned to choose between.

The Pro/Con List

Making a list of pros and cons, good and bad points about your top choices, may help you reach a decision. Imagine you've narrowed your list down to two possibilities: (1) buying your dad's Chevy; or (2) buying a used Honda. Try making a chart like this:

DAD'S CHEVY	
Pros	**Cons**
The price is right	Drive my dad's car (?)
New tires	Gas guzzler
No interest	Unexciting model
Known condition	Five years old

(Joe Duffy)

Make a similar list for the Honda. Then try to take an objective look at the strengths and weaknesses of each car.

There is nothing more to be esteemed than a manly firmness and decision of character. I like a person who knows his own mind and sticks to it; who sees at once what, in given circumstances is to be done, and does it.
—**William Hazlitt**

STEP 5. MAKE THE DECISION

The time will come when you must decide. Hopefully, the process has clarified your choices and shown you what to do. Some of us still drag our feet

119

and put off deciding as long as possible. Others tend to rush into everything. It will help you to know which way you lean.

Some people make decisions too quickly. If you're one of them, make yourself slow down. Don't come to snap decisions. Try to stay flexible as long as you can. You'll waste more time trying to undo a wrong decision.

Delaying a decision is not the same as indecision, however. Some people are too slow to decide. If that's you, then realize that many decisions can be changed quite easily. You have to move on something. It's easier to change directions of a moving vehicle than one stuck in the mud. Even if you make a mistake, it's probably not the end of the world.

TIPS ON DECISION MAKING

1. Clearly define the decision to be made.
2. Evaluate your decisions by your long-range goals.
3. Generate many possible decisions.
4. Evaluate each possible answer.
5. Make a list of pros and cons.
6. Know that, often you can change your mind.
7. Learn from your mistakes.

No Problem

Review the steps to problem solving:

Step 1. Identify and Define the Problem

Step 2. Define Goals and Objectives

Step 3. Generate Solutions

Step 4. Make a Plan of Action

Step 5. Follow Through

Don't forget that problems can turn into opportunities if you use both kinds of thinking—scientific and creative. Imagine the first guy who spilled bleach on his blue jeans and called it "stonewashed." Or, how about the fellow who ran from his bathtub, screaming, "Eureka!" when he figured out the displacement of water theory. Or Dr. Fleming, who returned to his lab and found a mold growing on a specimen slide. That problem turned into the discovery of penicillin.

Will you be one of those people who can say, "No problem" to difficulties? The decision is yours.

Men must be decided on what they will not do, and then they are able to act with vigor in what they ought to do.

—Mencius

EXERCISE

What's the biggest decision you're facing now? Run it through the five-step problem-solving process.

GLOSSARY

Brainstorming. The practice of quickly generating multiple ideas.

Clustering. Clustering, like free-word association, is a brainstorming technique to help spill out flashes of inspiration in unplanned relationships. Thoughts come out as clusters.

Contingency. Something that depends on unforeseen or accidental occurrences.

Convergent thinking. Logical, critical, analytical, straight-line, predictable thinking. Same as "scientific thinking."

Creative thinking. Inspirational, divergent, insightful, exploratory, unpredictable thinking. Creative thinking skyrockets you through new, provocative channels to shed light on new answers to old problems.

Divergent thinking. Same as "creative thinking."

Ex post facto. Faulty reasoning based on an assumed cause and effect.

Hasty generalization. The logical fallacy of assuming a connection between possibly unrelated events.

Hypothesis. An opinion or theory to be tested.

Logical fallacy. Errors in thinking.

Objectives. Usually small, specific steps that lead to a larger goal.

Poisoning the well. Hampering the credibility of someone before that person has an opportunity to present his or her case.

Problem-solving skills. Techniques that help clarify thinking and get to the root of problems, thus enabling an effective solution.

Scientific thinking. Logical, critical, analytical, convergent, straight-line, predictable thinking. It follows certain rules of logic from Point A through Point B to Point C.

Troubleshooting. Investigating, finding and wiping out the source of trouble.

Visualization. Creating a mental picture.

BIBLIOGRAPHY

Allison, Mike. *The Problem Buster's Guide.* Brookfield, VT: Ashgate Publishing Company, 1996.

Boice, James Montgomery. *An Expositional Commentary on Philippians.* Grand Rapids, Mich.: Zondervan Publishing House, 1971.

Bransford, John D. and Stein, Barry S. *The Ideal Problem Solver: A Guide for Improving Thinking, Learning, & Creativity.* New York: W.H. Freeman & Company, 1995.

Burns, Marilyn. *50 Problem Solving Lessons.* Reading, MA: Addison-Wesley Longman, Incorporated. 1995.

Greenes, Carole. *Strategies for Solving Problems (Spotlight on Understanding Series).* Dedham, MA: Janson Publications, 1996.

Michalko, Michael. *Thinkertoys: A Handbook of Business Creativity for the 90's.* Berkeley, Calif.: Ten Speed Press, 1991.

Paustian, Anthony. *Imagine!: Enhancing Your Problem-Solving & Critical Thinking Skills With Creativity.* Scarborough, ON Canada: Prentice Hall, 1996.

Raudsepp, Eugene. *Growth Games for the Creative Manager.* New York: Putnam, 1987.

Rico, Gabriele Lusser. *Writing the Natural Way.* Los Angeles: J.P. Tarcher, Inc., 1983.

Secretary's Commission on Achieving Necessary Skills. *Teaching the SCANS Competencies.* U.S. Department of Labor, 1993.

Wainwright, Gordon. *Essential Personal Skills for Life & Work.* Toronto: Pfeiffer & Co., 1993.

Winters, Nathan. *Creative Problem Solving.* Scarborough, ON Canada: Prentice Hall, 1996.

128